Nature's Cycles

The Food Cycle

Sally Morgan

WAYLAND

First published in 2008
by Wayland

Copyright © Wayland 2008

Wayland
338 Euston Road
London NW1 3BH

Wayland Australia
Level 17/207 Kent Street
Sydney, NSW 2000

Series editor: Nicola Edwards
Designer: Jason Billin

Picture acknowledgements: Cover main and title
Ecoscene/ Fritz Polking; scavenger with carrion
Ecoscene/ Bjorn Svensson; owl Ecoscene/ Frank
Blackburn; gerenuk Ecoscene/ Fritz Polking;p2
Ecoscene / Papilio / Gehan De Silva; p3 Ecoscene /
Papilio / Robert Pickett; p4 Ecoscene / Papilio / Tony
Wilson Bligh; p5 Ecoscene/ Wayne Lawler; p6
Ecoscene/ Sally Morgan; p7 Ecoscene/ NUR; p8
Ecoscene/ Fritz Polking; p9 Ecoscene / Papilio /
Robert Pickett; p10 Ecoscene/ Fritz Polking; p11 (t)
Ecoscene/ Fritz Polking, (b) Ecoscene/ Robin
Williams; p12 Ecoscene/ Satyendra Tiwari; p13
Ecoscene/ Michael Gore; p14 Ecoscene/ John Lewis;
p15 (t) Ecoscene / Papilio / Robert Pickett, (b)
Ecoscene / Papilio / Gehan De Silva; p16 Ecoscene/
Fritz Polking; p17 Ecoscene/ Reinhard Dirscherl; p18
Ecoscene/ Fritz Polking; p19 Ecoscene/ Anthony
Cooper; p20 Ecoscene / Papilio / Robert Pickett; p21
(t) Ecoscene/ Phillip Colla, (b) Ecoscene/ Reinhard
Dirscherl; p23 (t) Ecoscene / Papilio / Robert Pickett,
(b) Ecoscene/ Fritz Polking; p24 from top clockwise
Ecoscene/ Satyendra Tiwari - Ecoscene/ Bjorn
Svensson - Ecoscene/ Sally Morgan - Ecoscene/ Fritz
Polking; p25 Ecoscene/ Graham Neden; p26 Ecoscene/
Peter Cairns; p27 Ecoscene/ Nick Hawkes; p28
Ecoscene/ Andrew Brown; p29 (t) Ecoscene/ Anthony
Cooper, (b) Ecoscene/ Reinhard Dirscherl

Artwork by Jason Billin

British Library Cataloguing in Publication Data

Morgan, Sally
The food cycle. - (Nature's cycles)
1. Nutrient cycles - Juvenile literature 2. Food chains
(Biology) - Juvenile literature
I. Title
577.1'6

ISBN: 978 0 7502 5361 1

Printed in China

Wayland is a division of Hachette Children's Books,
an Hachette Livre UK company.

Contents

Living together

Imagine looking out over the African savannah. There are herds of grazing animals such as zebra, antelope and wildebeest. Predators such as lions and cheetahs watch from the top of rocky outcrops, and vultures fly overhead. Lizards bask on the rocks while snakes hide away from the sun. All these animals are living together in the same habitat. Together with the plants they form a community.

▶ During the dry season many grazing animals such as elephants, zebra and springbok visit this waterhole to drink. This attracts predators such as lions.

Feeding relationships

The members of a community can be grouped according to their role. Plants, which can make their own food, belong to a group called producers. Animals are unable to make their own food, so they rely on 'ready-made' food in the form of plants and other animals. Animals that eat the producers are called primary consumers. Secondary consumers are animals that eat the primary consumers, and tertiary consumers eat the secondary consumers. The producers and consumers are linked together in a relationship called a food chain. Food chains are linked together in a food web. When one organism eats another, energy is transferred from one to the other. When organisms die, they are decomposed, or broken down, by decomposers such as bacteria and fungi.

In Focus: Capturing energy

All food chains start with the capture of energy and its conversion to a form that organisms can use. On land, most food chains rely on plants to capture light energy and use it to make foods that animals can use. Many bacteria are producers. Some use light energy while others use chemical energy locked up in various substances to fuel their growth.

▶ Elephants spend up to 18 hours a day grazing on twigs, bark and leaves. They use their long trunks to reach the higher branches.

Recycling food

Food chains are all about energy and nutrients. At each stage, energy and nutrients are transferred between one organism and the next in the food chain. Plants are producers and they use energy from the sun and nutrients from the ground to grow. When these producers are eaten, energy and nutrients are transferred to the primary consumers. At the end of a food chain, the decomposers return the nutrients to the ground to be recycled, but the energy is lost to the environment. In this book you can learn about the food cycle: the process by which energy and nutrients are passed along the food chain and then the nutrients are recycled to be used all over again.

In Focus: Biodiversity

Scientists often refer to biodiversity. This is the total number of different plants and animals living in a particular habitat. Tropical rainforests have the largest biodiversity of all habitats. Only about six per cent of the world's land surface is covered by these forests but half of all the different types of plants and animals live in them.

The producers

Plants are the producers of virtually all the food chains on land, and most in the sea. In the sea, the producers include seaweeds and tiny single-celled organisms called phytoplankton. In a few food chains bacteria are the producers.

⬤ Plants position their leaves so they can intercept as much light as possible.

Plants and photosynthesis

Plants are green because their leaves contain a green pigment called chlorophyll. Chlorophyll traps light energy and uses it to combine carbon dioxide and water to make sugar and oxygen. This process is called photosynthesis. The carbon dioxide comes from the air while the water is taken up by the plant's roots and carried to its leaves.

Investigate: Eating five-a-day

Plant foods are an essential part of a healthy diet. Experts recommend that everybody eats at least five portions of vegetables or fruits every day. Do you? Keep a food diary for a week and make a note of every portion of fruit and vegetables that you eat. A portion is a single piece of fruit, a glass of fruit juice, or a handful of dried fruits such as raisins, or of peas, carrots or other fresh or frozen vegetables.

Air contains about 21 per cent oxygen. All the oxygen comes from plants. Virtually all organisms need oxygen to survive. When humans breathe in oxygen it is carried by the blood to all parts of the body. In the human body, oxygen is used in a process called respiration in which sugar is broken down into carbon dioxide, water and energy. The carbon dioxide is carried in the blood back to the lungs and then it is exhaled. Plants need carbon dioxide for photosynthesis and oxygen too, for respiration. Plants make more oxygen than they use, providing an essential source of oxygen for humans and other animals.

The sugars made by photosynthesis can be turned into a range of substances such as fats and proteins that are needed by the plant. Any excess sugar is transported down the stem to the root where it is converted to starch and stored for future use.

Producers under the sea

Thousands of metres under the sea there are cracks in the seabed where very hot water gushes out. Here, scientists have discovered a very strange community of animals that are found nowhere else on Earth. No light reaches the seabed, so the producers there are bacteria. They obtain their energy from chemicals in the water. The bacteria are eaten by animals such as giant tube worms.

▶ These giant tube worms are found around a hot water vent. They grow to one metre in length.

The plant eaters

Plants are eaten by many different primary consumers. These are the plant-eating animals, or herbivores.

Cellulose

Plant foods can be tough and difficult to digest. This is because they contain large amounts of a type of carbohydrate called cellulose. Herbivores have various ways of dealing with cellulose. Most herbivores have large teeth that chew plant foods into a pulp with saliva, making it easier to digest. For example, animals such as sheep and horses have large, flat, ridged molars at the back of the mouth, which grind food into small pieces.

Rabbits and other herbivores have a very long gut so food takes a long time to pass through it. This allows plenty of time for their bodies to digest the cellulose they have eaten. Rabbits produce two types of droppings, dry brown ones and green ones, which contain water and partially-digested plant material. They eat the green droppings so that the plant material they contain can pass through the digestive system a second time.

◖ The gerenuk is a browsing herbivore with a long neck. It stands on its back legs to reach the higher branches that are out of reach of other antelopes.

Ruminants

Mammals cannot digest cellulose, so many plant-eating mammals called ruminants have micro-organisms living in their gut that can digest it for them. Ruminants, such as sheep, antelopes and cattle, have a huge stomach containing four chambers. The animals chew their food and swallow it. After an hour or so they bring the food back up into their mouth for a second time. This is called 'chewing the cud' and it makes sure that the grass is well chewed. Then the food passes through into the next chamber of the stomach where lots of micro-organisms break down the cellulose so that the nutrients can be absorbed.

Investigate: Compost heaps

Gardeners build compost heaps where fungi and other micro-organisms break down the garden waste. As the waste is broken down a lot of heat is released. You can test this for yourself. Make a pile of grass clippings and after a day feel the surface – it should feel warm. You could measure the temperature inside the heap with a thermometer over a week.

🔻 Each leaf cutter ant carries a cut-out piece of leaf back to its nest to feed the fungi there.

In Focus: Leaf cutter ants

Leaf cutter ants leave their nest each day to search for food. They use their jaws to cut out pieces of leaves that they carry back to their nest. They cannot digest cellulose, so they farm fungi that can digest it. They dig an underground chamber where they grow the fungi. These chambers are called fungal gardens. The ants feed the leaves to the fungi. The leaves are broken down and digested by the fungi and then the ants eat the fungi, creating a mini food chain.

The carnivores

The next stage in the food cycle happens when primary consumers are eaten by secondary consumers, the carnivores. These are the animals that eat other animals. These meat-eating animals are also described as predators. They range in size from microscopic one-celled organisms that live in water to the largest animal on the planet, the blue whale.

▶ Mammals, such as this water buffalo, allow oxpeckers to remove parasites such as ticks and mites from their skin.

Special senses

There are many different types of predator and each has a different way of capturing its food and eating it. A predator relies on its senses to find its prey. For example, birds of prey and frogs have excellent eyesight and they can spot the slightest movement of another animal. A pit viper, a type of snake, has a special sense that detects the body heat of its prey so it can hunt in the dark. Bats use echolocation to 'see' in the dark. They emit high frequency sounds that bounce off objects in their path, creating echoes that the bats can hear.

In Focus: Parasites

A parasite is an organism that feeds on another organism, called a host, and does harm to that organism. For example, a tapeworm is a long flat worm that lives in the gut of another animal, such as a pig. The tapeworm absorbs food from the gut of the host animal. Eventually the host dies of starvation. Some parasites, such as mites and ticks, live on the outside of a host and suck its blood. Many human diseases such as malaria that occur in tropical parts of the world are caused by parasites.

Teeth and claws

Predators need to be able to catch, hold and then kill their prey. Many predators have powerful beaks or jaws, and claws to grip an animal they have caught. The tiger for example, leaps onto its prey, such as a deer, and pulls it to the ground, holding it down with its claws. Then it clamps its jaws on the animal's neck and bites through it.

▶ This osprey has caught a fish in its hooked talons and is flying back to its perch to eat it.

Laying traps

Some predators lie in wait for their prey to pass close by and others lay traps. For example, orb web spiders spin webs with sticky threads that trap flying insects, while trap door spiders hide in their burrow and leap out to catch their prey.

Investigate: Spider's webs

Orb web spiders usually spin a fresh web every day. First they eat the old threads and then they spin new ones. Any insect that becomes entangled is paralysed and then wrapped up in silk. Find a spider's web in a garden or garage and check that there is a spider living in the web. Over a week, go out each day to see if the spider has caught any animals or repaired its web.

◀ This spider has caught a fly and packaged it up in silk threads to eat later.

11

The top carnivores

The last carnivore in a food chain is called the top carnivore. In a short food chain, there may only be a plant, a herbivore and a carnivore. However in longer food chains the secondary consumer in a food chain may be preyed upon by another carnivore, the tertiary consumer. In a few food chains there is yet another carnivore preying on the tertiary consumer in the chain (see pages 4-5).

Large and few

The top carnivores tend to be large animals and they are few in number. For example, the tiger is the top carnivore of the Indian jungle. Usually there are only one or two tigers in an area of jungle of about 100 square kilometres. The tigers prey on herbivores such as deer, antelope and pigs. It takes a tiger time and energy to catch its prey and many hunts are unsuccessful. Therefore, it tends to catch animals that are at least half its size, so that there is enough meat to last the tiger several days. If it hunted only small animals, it would have to catch more of them.

▼ This tiger has caught a sambar, a type of deer, which it drags into the forest to eat.

Investigate: Carnivores

Look on the Internet or visit a local library to find the answers to these questions. Can you name two top carnivores that can be found on African savannah? Name a top carnivore that is found in a marine habitat.

12

Brown bears and polar bears are also top carnivores. In autumn in North America, brown bears are seen hunting along rivers where they catch salmon, a predatory fish. The bear has powerful claws which it uses to grip the salmon's slippery body. Polar bears hunt seals which in turn prey on fish. The polar bears use their weight to smash a hole through the ice and then they sit patiently by the hole waiting for a seal to come to the surface.

⚠ For a few weeks each year, brown bears in North America catch salmon as they make their way up rivers to their breeding grounds.

An exception to the rule

Humans have few enemies, so in many food chains the human is the top carnivore, eating, for example, fish and beef. However, humans are not necessarily larger than the animals they eat, nor are there fewer humans. This is because we humans use tools such as guns, enabling us to kill animals much larger than ourselves, and have more sources of food available to us.

In Focus: Predators and prey

There is an important relationship between the numbers of predators and their prey. If the number of prey increases, there is more food for the predators. They raise more young and their number increases. If the number of prey decreases, so too does the number of predators because they run out of food.

However, the changes do not happen at the same time. First there is a change in the number of prey, and after a while there is a change in the number of predators.

Avoiding predators

Prey animals have developed many ways of escaping from their predators to avoid becoming food!

Poisonous animals

Many animals are poisonous so other animals avoid eating them. This means that poisonous animals are at the end of a food chain as they are not eaten. For example, the monarch butterfly is poisonous because its caterpillar eats milkweed, a poisonous plant. Both the caterpillar and the adult butterfly advertise their poison with bright warning colours. Rainforest frogs are preyed upon by snakes and birds. However, the brightly coloured poison arrow frog is a top carnivore in the forest. It is incredibly poisonous so no animal dares to eat it.

In Focus: Clever disguise

Another way of avoiding a predator is by using camouflage. Camouflage is a pattern of colours that blends in with the surroundings, such as tiger stripes in dappled shade in forests. If a camouflaged animal remains still, it is incredibly difficult to spot. Some animals have a body that is shaped to look like an object, for example the buff tip moth looks like a bit of twig, while the leafy dragon looks like a piece of seaweed.

⊙ The leafy dragon doesn't look like a fish. It has lots of leaf-like attachments to disguise its shape.

Copycats

Some animals mimic the colours of a poisonous animal so that they look almost identical to it. The mimic aims to fool predators into thinking that it is poisonous so that they will leave it alone. For example, hoverflies are harmless insects but they look remarkably like wasps that sting.
The viceroy butterfly mimics the bright colours of the monarch. Its disguise is so good that it can be difficult to tell the monarch and viceroy apart.

⬤ Many butterflies copy the orange and black colours of the poisonous monarch butterfly.

Living in groups

Some animals have found that living together means that they are less likely to be caught by a predator. The meerkats of southern Africa live together in colonies. One or two meerkats are continually on guard duty, watching for predators. They warn the others so that they all have a chance of reaching safety before a predator such as a bird of prey gets too close. Fish in shoals are safer from predators than fish living on their own. When fish move together in a shoal, they confuse a predator such as a shark or dolphin, which finds it difficult to follow an individual fish.

⬤ Meerkats on guard duty stand on rocky outcrops to get a good view of the surrounding grassland.

Investigate: Camouflage

Take a large piece of paper and paint it black. Add some white spots of differing sizes at random. Now cut out a fish shape from a second piece of paper. Paint it black and add some white spots. Place the cut out shape on the paper. The shape should blend with the background and be difficult to spot.

Numbers and biomass

If you were to count all the individual organisms at each feeding level in a food chain, you would find that there were more at the bottom than at the top.

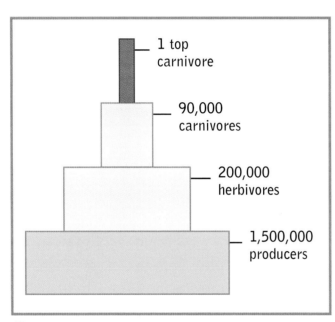

- 1 top carnivore
- 90,000 carnivores
- 200,000 herbivores
- 1,500,000 producers

⬆ This diagram shows a simple pyramid of numbers.

Pyramids of numbers

The level with the largest number of individuals is the producer level at the bottom of the food chain. The next largest number relates to the primary consumers. As you go up the chain there are fewer and fewer animals. The highest level, that of the top carnivores, has the smallest number of animals. The reason for the decline is simple. There cannot be more predators than prey. If there were, then all the prey animals would be eaten. So as a general rule, there are fewer animals at each level in the food chain.

This change in number can be shown on a special graph called a pyramid of numbers. The pyramid is made up of horizontal bars, with each bar representing a feeding level. The width of the bar shows the number of individuals in that feeding level. The bar at the bottom is the widest.

◀ In a pyramid of numbers, one rhino and one egret are counted as the same, although they differ greatly in mass.

16

Investigate: Leaf litter

Leaf litter is full of tiny animals, both herbivores and carnivores. Collect some leaf litter in a bucket from under a tree. Tip it out onto a large white sheet spread on the ground. Collect the animals using a small artist's brush and place them in a see-through container with a lid. Using a guidebook, see if you can identify which animals are herbivores and which carnivores. How many of each kind are there? Once you have finished, place all the animals and the leaf litter back under the tree.

Pyramids of biomass

The pyramid of numbers makes no allowance for size. For example, when you count herbivores, an elephant counts as one but so does a grasshopper, although the elephant has thousands of times more mass. A more realistic way of looking at the food chain, is to look at the mass of all the living organisms in a feeding level, that is, the mass of all the producers, the mass of the primary consumers, and so on. The biomass (the living mass) of an organism represents both the number and the size of the organism. If the biomass of the different levels was plotted on a graph, this graph would be a pyramid too.

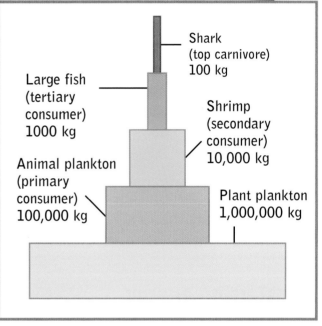

Shark (top carnivore) 100 kg

Large fish (tertiary consumer) 1000 kg

Shrimp (secondary consumer) 10,000 kg

Animal plankton (primary consumer) 100,000 kg

Plant plankton 1,000,000 kg

⭕ This diagram shows a simple pyramid of biomass for a marine food chain (see pages 20-21).

🔻 A jellyfish is more than 95% water and floats in the upper layer of water.

In Focus: Energy

A third way of displaying a food chain is as a pyramid of energy. This is even more accurate than using biomass. It takes into account the amount of energy locked up in the plants and animals. For example, a jellyfish may weigh a lot but it is mostly water, whereas a fish may have lots of energy-rich fat in its body.

Energy and food chains

Energy is very important in food chains because organisms need energy to grow and reproduce. It is needed at the start of the food chain and it is passed from one organism to another along the food chain.

Capturing energy

At the start of the food chain the plants trap light energy from the sun. However they only trap a tiny fraction of the light that falls on their leaves. The rest of the light is either reflected away or passes straight through the leaf. Plants convert the light energy into chemical energy. The rest of the energy is used to fuel their growth but some is lost as heat energy when the cells respire.

Transferring energy

When an animal eats a plant, the energy locked up in the plant is transferred to the animal. However, less than 15 per cent of the energy locked up in a plant is used by the animal in growth and the production of new biomass. The rest of the energy is lost in many ways. Firstly, an animal does not usually eat all of a plant. Some energy is left behind in stems and roots. Also some leaves may have died before an animal eats them. More energy is lost in the animal's gut because some of the plant cannot be digested. Energy remains locked up in the undigested parts, which are passed out in droppings.

▼ A cheetah uses energy as it chases its prey at high speeds.

18

Energy is also lost when a carnivore eats a herbivore, as just 10 to 15 per cent of the energy locked up in the body of the herbivore is passed to the carnivore and used in growth. The rest of the energy is wasted. For example, the carnivore may not eat skin and bones and it may not digest all the food that passes through its gut. Also, heat is produced when the animal runs around looking for food and this too wastes energy.

So at every stage in the food chain, only a fraction of the energy in one level is passed to the next.

⬤ These caterpillars have only eaten part of the leaf, the tough bits have been left behind.

In Focus: Should we eat meat?

Eating meat is energy-expensive. A lot of energy is lost when animals are raised for meat. For example, a farmer has to grow crops such as wheat and peas that are used to feed beef cattle. The cattle only gain about 10 to 15 per cent of the energy in their food. In turn, when people eat beef there is a lot of wasted energy because the skin and bones are not eaten. Overall, only about one per cent of the energy locked in the original crop reaches people. Some people argue that, if everyone were to eat a vegetarian diet, less energy would be wasted. People would eat the crops directly and would gain 10 to 15 per cent of the energy locked up in crops. However, other people argue that humans are neither herbivores like zebras, or carnivores like lions. Humans are omnivores and our teeth and gut are designed to eat a mix of plant and animal foods.

Marine food chains

The oceans are home to many different types of plants and animals, all adapted to living in water. Most live in the uppermost layer of water where there is plenty of light. Some of the longest food chains are found in the oceans. This is because the chains are efficient and more energy passes from level to level. For example, a seal will eat a whole fish, not just part of it, so there is less waste.

Plankton and krill

At the bottom of a marine food chain are the producers, the plant plankton and the seaweeds. Plant plankton float in the water and use light to photosynthesise. They are eaten by animal plankton. These are mostly floating animals such as the larvae of fish and crabs, jellyfish, and small crustaceans called copepods. The more plankton there is in the ocean, the more food there is for the plankton eaters – the fish and other marine animals. Another important marine animal is krill. These are small shrimps, which occur in huge shoals. They feed on plankton and in turn are preyed upon by many fish and whales.

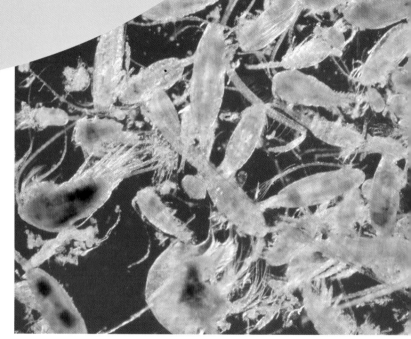

⬤ Plankton is made up of microscopic organisms such as these tiny shrimp-like animals.

Investigate: Fish

Three common types of fish on sale in shops are plaice, sardines and tuna. Can you find out what these three types of fish eat? Which predators eat them? Where would you place them in a food chain?

20

Predators

There are many predators in the ocean, such as tuna and marlin, sharks, seals, dolphins and killer whales. A large shoal of a small fish such as sardines attracts predators. The predators surround the shoal and then swim through it, trying to separate out some of the fish to make them easier to catch. A shoal also attracts predatory sea birds such as cormorants and gannets that dive into the water to catch fish.

◀ Seals and sea lions are predators. This sea lion is chasing a puffer fish.

In Focus: Coral reefs

Coral reefs are home to more marine plants and animals than any other marine habitat. The reefs are found in warm waters where the water is clear and unpolluted. They are built by corals, animals that look like tiny sea anemones. Each coral animal builds a skeleton around its body and when it dies the skeleton is left behind and forms the coral rock. Over a very long period of time, a coral reef builds up. Hiding in the reef are many different invertebrate animals such as clams, crabs, prawns and starfish. They attract fish, turtles and other predators.

▶ The powerful beak of the turtle enables it to break off and eat lumps of hard coral.

Food webs

A food chain shows how one animal is eaten by another and energy is passed along. However, it's not quite that simple! It is unusual for one animal to eat just one type of food. Most animals eat a variety of foods. A more realistic way to show the relationship between all the plants and animals in the food cycle is by drawing a food web.

A food web

A food chain can be shown on a piece of paper as a series of plants and animals linked by arrows which indicate the transfer of energy. A food web is the same but far more complex. There are several links between the different animals, showing what they eat. Some carnivores may feed on four or five different types of herbivores and the herbivore may feed on a range of plants. All these links have to be shown by an arrow.

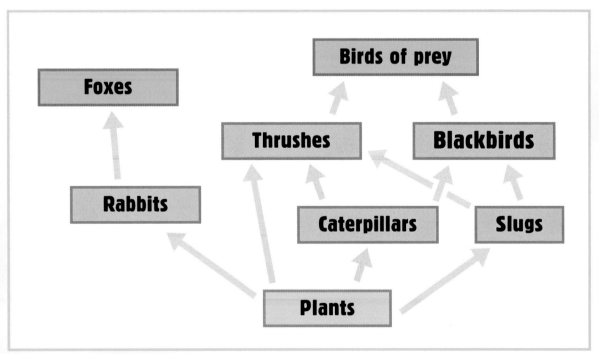

⬤ This diagram shows a simple food web.

⦿ The ladybird is an important predator in the garden because it feeds on greenflies or aphids, a pest of many plants.

Food security

It is important that animals do not rely too much on one or two sources of food. If anything were to happen to that food source, they would run out of food and starve. For example, a disease or a natural disaster such as a flood or drought could remove their only source of food. Animals that eat a variety of foods are more likely to survive times of food shortages as they can look for an alternative food source. The world's cities are full of animals that are very adaptable. Many have lost their natural habitats but they have adapted to a new range of foods available in cities, including food in rubbish bins.

⦿ The most important food for the puffin is the sand eel. If there are not enough sand eels the number of puffins falls.

Nature's dustmen

The food cycle does not end when an organism dies. There is a lot of energy locked up in a fallen leaf or a dead body. Rather than let this energy go to waste, another group of organisms – the decomposers – feeds on the dead and decaying material.

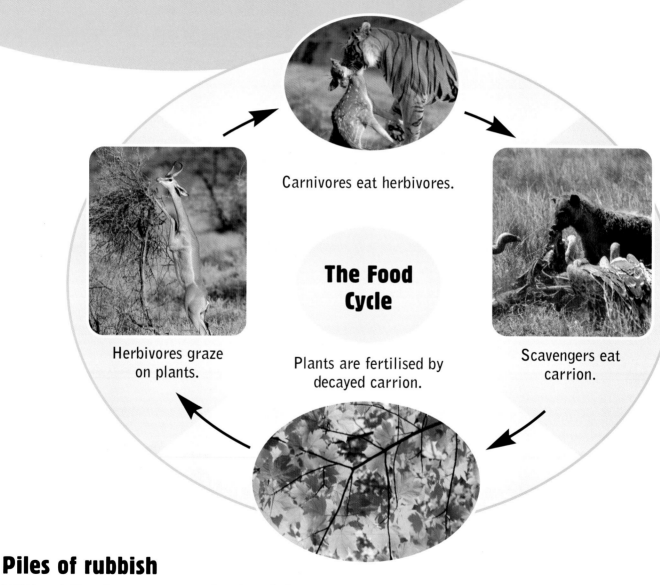

The Food Cycle

Carnivores eat herbivores.

Herbivores graze on plants.

Plants are fertilised by decayed carrion.

Scavengers eat carrion.

Piles of rubbish

Without the decomposers, dead and decaying matter would build up in habitats. Grasslands would be littered with rotting bodies and piles of animal dung, while forests would have thick layers of dead leaves and fallen branches carpeting the ground.

Feeding on waste

First, the dead material is eaten by larger organisms such as slugs, snails and earthworms. They eat the dead material and break it down into smaller pieces. Flies lay their eggs on dead bodies and these hatch into maggots that feed on the decaying material. Then the smaller decomposers get to work. These are micro-organisms such as bacteria and fungi. They break down the remaining dead material into nutrients. They use some of these nutrients in their own growth, but the rest are returned to the soil. Here, they are taken up by plant roots and the food cycle begins again.

▽ A fresh piece of dung on the ground is soon surrounded by dung beetles that break it up, form it into small balls and push it away.

In Focus: Dung beetles

One of the most important decomposers on grassland is the dung beetle. This small beetle loves animal dung, especially that from grazing animals, because it is full of nutrients. Dung beetles use their excellent sense of smell to detect a fresh pile of dung. They shape the dung into small balls and push it over the ground to a small hole. It is stored in the ground as a food larder. Many dung beetles lay their eggs in the dung. When the larvae hatch they have a ready-made supply of food.

Investigate: Keeping worms

You can watch how worms feed on fallen leaves by keeping them in a wormery for a week or two. Take a two-litre sized clear plastic bottle and cut off the top. Fill the bottle with soil mixed with a bit of sand. Make sure it is damp. Add a layer of leaves to the top and wrap dark paper around the bottle. Now your wormery is ready for some worms. Add a four or five earthworms to the top. They will quickly disappear into the soil. Leave the wormery in a cool place out of the sun. Every few days remove the paper and look for signs of worms. After a couple of weeks, release your worms back outside.

Food from field to plate

People are an important part of the food cycle because we need food just as animals do. Today, the world's population stands at 6 billion and it is rising all the time. This means that vast amounts of food are needed each day to keep everybody alive.

⬥ These free range chickens can leave their barn and roam over the field during the day.

First farmers

Early people hunted animals for meat and collected fruits and seeds from the wild. The people were part of the food web. Then, about 10,000 years ago, people started to farm. Land was cleared to grow crops such as wheat and animals were tamed. People kept chickens, goats and sheep to provide eggs, milk and meat.

Clearing land

Over the last few hundred years, large areas of the world's grasslands have been ploughed up to provide land for farming. Forests too have been cleared to provide more land for keeping animals. All this farming activity has had a severe effect on the natural habitats.

Today, crop yields are boosted by adding fertilisers to the soil to supply plenty of nutrients. Farmers protect their crops by spraying them with pesticides and weedkillers, but these chemicals harm the environment. Some pesticides kill useful insects and birds, while fertilisers run off the land into streams and rivers and harm aquatic life.

In Focus: Organic farming

Organic farming is a way of farming without using artificial fertilisers and pesticides, but relying on natural methods. Organic farmers tend to keep traditional breeds of animals that live outside rather than crowded together inside barns. This style of farming is environmentally friendly which means that more wildlife can survive on the farmland.

◐ A farmers market is a place where shoppers can buy foods produced by local farmers.

Energy and farming

Energy is used at all stages in the food cycle. Energy is used to make fertilisers and pesticides, and tractors use energy when they spread chemicals over the crops and harvest them. Yet more energy is used to take the crops to processing plants where they are made into animal feed or food for people. Then more energy is used to transport the food to shops.

Investigate: Food miles

Wander around a supermarket and you will see foods from all parts of the world. For example, mangoes, bananas and pineapples from tropical parts of the world, fish from the Pacific and vegetables from Egypt. Transporting food, especially by air, uses up a great deal of energy. It is more environmentally friendly to buy food that is grown locally, rather rely on foods that have been flown half way round the world. Look at the labels on the foods in your kitchen. Where did the food come from? How much of it was grown locally? Can you work out the food miles for the foods used to prepare one meal?

Disrupted food cycles

It is very easy to upset the balance of the food cycle. Natural events such as fires, floods and droughts can cause disruption. But a more common cause is the activities of people.

Hunting

There is always a small number of top carnivores (see pages 12-13), so hunting can soon threaten their survival. If numbers of top carnivores fall, the whole food cycle can be disrupted. For example, big cats such as the leopard, cheetah and tiger have been hunted for their attractive fur. Their numbers have fallen greatly, for example there are probably fewer than 5,000 Bengal tigers in the wild and even fewer snow leopards. When the top carnivore is removed, there are fewer predators to prey on the smaller animals and they increase in number. The more of the smaller animals there are, the more plant food is needed, so grassland may become overgrazed.

⬤ Within this small area of a rainforest it is possible to spot many different species of plants.

Investigate: Food webs

For this investigation you will need some reference books or access to the Internet. Imagine all the zebras on an African savannah were removed. Can you work out what effect this would have on the food web? Which herbivores would increase in number? What would happen to the predators?

Habitat loss

More people means there is more demand for land for farming, industry, homes and roads. Around the world, habitats are being cleared causing major disruption to food chains. One habitat of particular importance is the tropical rainforest with its huge biodiversity. For example, in one 10-hectare plot of Malaysian rainforest scientists have found 780 species of trees. Living on these trees were thousands of species of animals. If this plot of forest were cleared, all these plants and animals would lose their homes. The plants would die and the animals would move away.

Recreating food chains

It is possible to repair land that has been damaged, for example, by restoring farmland to become species-rich meadows. However it is more difficult to create rainforest as it takes so long to grow.

It is also possible to re-introduce species into a habitat. For example, the Great bustard, a large bird, disappeared from Britain during the 1830s. These birds are being reintroduced as their habitat is now protected and they have a chance of survival. There are even suggestions that the wolf and beaver could be re-introduced to Scotland. In the United States the Mexican wolf, Californian condor and black-footed ferret are just three species that have been reintroduced to their former habitats.

In 1998, 11 Mexican wolves were successfully released into protected areas of Arizona and New Mexico in the United States.

This wreck of a plane is now home to many different fish and corals are beginning to grow.

In Focus: Recreating coral reefs

A number of new coral reefs have been established around the world. Corals need something to grow on so people have sunk old warships, cars and even tyres. Within a surprisingly short time of a few years, many communities of coral animals have become established and fish have moved into the area.

Glossary

adapted Suited.

aquatic Living in water.

bacteria Microscopic micro-organisms too small to be seen by the eye alone.

biodiversity The total number of plants and animals that are living in a particular habitat.

biomass The living mass of an organism.

camouflage A pattern of colouring that blends with the background.

carbon dioxide A gas found in the atmosphere. We breathe in oxygen and breathe out carbon dioxide.

carnivore An animal that eats meat.

cell The smallest unit of a living organism. Plants are made up of millions of cells.

cellulose A substance made from sugar that is found in the cell wall of all plant cells.

chlorophyll The green pigment in plants.

community A group of plants and animals living in the same habitat.

copepod A tiny shrimp-like animal that lives in water.

decomposer An organism that brings about decay.

echolocation A system that uses sound to find objects in the air or water, used by bats and dolphins.

energy Organisms need energy to move and grow.

fertiliser A substance that is added to soil to provide plants with the nutrients that they need to grow well.

food chain A sequence of organisms in which energy is transferred from one organism to the next.

food web Interconnected food chains.

fungal garden An underground chamber in which termites or leaf cutter ants grow fungi to feed on.

herbivore An animal that eats plants.

host An organism on which a parasite lives and feeds. The host eventually dies from starvation.

invertebrate An animal that does not have a backbone.

krill Marine shrimp-like animals that live in large shoals.

marine To do with the sea.

micro-organism A tiny organism that is too small to see by the eye alone.

mimic To copy.

molars A type of large tooth at the back of the mouth.

nutrient A substance needed for healthy growth.

parasite An organism that lives in or on another organism and causes harm to that organism.

pesticides Substances that are used to kill certain types of pests, such as insects or fungi.

photosynthesis The process by which a plant makes sugar and oxygen from carbon dioxide and water in the presence of light.

plankton Microscopic plants and animals that float in the upper layers of the water.

predator An animal that hunts other animals.

prey Animals that are hunted by other animals.

primary consumer The first consumer in the food chain, an animal that eats producers.

producers Living things, such as plants and bacteria, that can make their own food. Producers are at the bottom of any food chain.

proteins Substances found in food that organisms need to grow and thrive.

respiration The process that takes place in cells, by which sugar is broken down into carbon dioxide and water with the release of energy.

ruminant A herbivore with a specialised stomach containing micro-organisms that digest cellulose.

savannah Tropical grassland that is flat with few trees.

secondary consumer The second consumer in the food chain, an animal that eats primary consumers.

starch A carbohydrate that is made by plants.

sugar A sweet-tasting carbohydrate.

tertiary consumer The third consumer in a food chain, an animal that eats secondary consumers.

top carnivore The last carnivore in a food chain that is not preyed upon by other animals.

Further Information

Books

How we use plants for food, Sally Morgan, Wayland, 2007

I wonder why caterpillars eat so much and other questions about life cycles, Belinda Weber, Kingfisher, 2006

Sea hunters: dolphins, whales and seals, Andrew Solway, Heinemann Library, 2006

Websites

Food for a healthy planet
http://www.climatechoices.org.uk/pages/food0.htm
Find out how you can calculate the food miles for different meals

5-a-day
http://www.5aday.nhs.uk
Find out more about eating more fruit and vegetables

Index